SCHOOL to HOME

TRANSITIONING TO HOME EDUCATION

ENCOURAGEMENT FOR THE CHRISTIAN PARENT

Effie Hill

light-on-a-hill.com

Light on a Hill Publishing

ISBN: 978-1-105-53023-4

Illustrations by Patrick J. Hill

ALL RIGHTS RESERVED. No part of this publication may be reproduced, stored in a retrieval system or transmitted in any form or by any means, electronic, mechanical, photocopying, recording or otherwise, without the prior permission of the author or illustrator.

Scripture quotations marked "NKJV™" are taken from the New King James Version®. Copyright © 1982 by Thomas Nelson, Inc. Used by permission. All rights reserved.

THE HOLY BIBLE, NEW INTERNATIONAL VERSION®, NIV® Copyright © 1973, 1978, 1984, 2011 by Biblica, Inc.™ Used by permission. All rights reserved worldwide.

To my precious saplings—
Jacob, Avyi, and Elijah

TABLE OF CONTENTS

Introduction / page 7

Chapter 1 / page 15
   Our Journey Begins

Chapter 2 / page 23
   Transplant Shock (Part 1)—Expect the Transition to be Challenging

Chapter 3 / page 33
   Transplant Shock (Part 2)—Challenges from Within

Chapter 4 / page 45
   Transplant Shock (Part 3)—Challenges from Without

Chapter 5 / page 53
   Add Some Sugar—Help the Children See the Benefits

Chapter 6 / page 63
   Acclimation—Adjusting to the New Soil

Chapter 7 / page 79
   Enlist Assistance and Seek Support

Chapter 8 / page 85
   Keep the Soil Moist—Nourishment in the Home

Chapter 9 / page 97
   Consult the Master Gardener and Wait Patiently for the Harvest

Additional Resources / page 107

INTRODUCTION

The famous statistician, W.A. Wallis, once said that "statistics may be defined as 'a body of methods for making wise decisions in the face of uncertainty.'" If you are uncertain about the decision to homeschool or you are sitting on the fence, a quick look at the latest statistics regarding public schools quickly reveals a broken system of education. Academically, the United States trails behind many other Western nations despite spending more money per student. According to the National Assessment of Educational Progress (NAEP) data, 34 percent of fourth-graders, 30 percent of eighth-graders, and only 21 percent of twelfth-graders performed at or above the *proficient* level in science in 2009 (1). NAEP data also found that only 33 percent of fourth-graders and 32 percent of eighth-graders performed at the proficient level in reading! (2)

These academic failures are just the tip of the iceberg. During the 2007–2008 school year, 85 percent of public schools recorded that incidents of violence, theft, or other crimes had taken place; which translates to a rate of 43 crimes per 1,000 students. (3) Furthermore, approximately one quarter of students in 2009 reported that someone either offered, gave, or sold drugs to them. (4) In 2007, around one third of students aged 12 to 18 years reported they were victims of bullying. (5)

With the statistics pointing to a floundering public school system in the United States, many Christian parents are no longer wavering between sending their precious children to public schools versus homeschooling them. They are opting for a wiser choice—the option to educate their children at home. More importantly, many parents are realizing that there is no neutral worldview and that public schools are actually making a loud statement by keeping silent about God during a child's education. Seventy-five percent of children from Christian homes who have attended public school will turn away from their faith during their first year of college. However, less than 4 percent of homeschooled children will do so. (6) With the latest numbers supporting not only the academic, but the spiritual benefits of homeschooling, objectively measured results have propelled a once-fringe schooling option into the mainstream.

Our own children never attended public schools. We opted for private Christian school, considering it to be an acceptable alternative. I will elaborate more in the first chapter, but we experienced first-hand that there is often little difference between public and private schooling. When I would hear some of the statistics mentioned above, I would think that people were choosing to keep their children at home out of fear. However, in due time, I realized that these numbers point to a greater spiritual truth, and that is why there are so many problems; institutionalized schooling, whether public or private, does not afford the *best* opportunity to a Christian family to fulfill the Biblical commandment for parents to teach their children God's ways (Deuteronomy 6:6-7).

In addition, the Bible says that foolishness is bound up in the heart of a child and that discipline will drive it out (Proverbs 22:15). Gathering foolish children together, outside of parental jurisdiction, can only lead to problems.

In his book, *Homeschooling from a Biblical Worldview*, Israel Wayne puts it best: "Traditional classroom teaching is a man-made, artificial substitute invented to excuse us from fulfilling our God-given responsibility to teach our own children. It is critical that we come to a place of Biblical conviction concerning God's perfect will." *(7)* He describes homeschooling as a response to God—not a reaction to public school.

Many parents have reached the same conclusion, leading to a rapid increase in homeschooling. A survey by the Department of Education's *National Center for Education Statistics* reveals that in 2007, 1.5 million children were learning at home—an increase of 75 percent since 1999. In its summary, the report cites that parents homeschooled their children for a variety of reasons, but it noted three as most important: concern regarding the school environment, including reasons such as safety, drugs or negative peer pressure *(88 percent); a* desire to provide religious or moral instruction *(83 percent); and* dissatisfaction with academic instruction at other schools *(73 percent). (8)*

Whether transitioning from public or private school to educating at home, both pose unique challenges that must be faced—challenges that one does not encounter if a child has never been mass-schooled, but has been educated at home from the beginning. Many parents find these challenges so daunting that they never make the change to homeschooling.

During my initial research into homeschooling, I found tidbits of advice about transitioning, but never an entire book dedicated to the subject. After several years of a challenging but successful transition for our family, and after talking to others that were struggling with the decisions and the "how to" of removing their children from public or private school, I decided that other people facing this transition might glean from our mistakes and victories. I wish I had been handed a manual that offered suggestions for overcoming some of the initial hurdles, or described what problems to anticipate; therefore I chose to write this book.

My prayer and goal is that *School to Home* will serve as a guide and encouragement for those brave parents that take a leap of faith and decide to do what is best—grow their children in the fertile soil of the home—so that these precious ones truly are like thriving olive plants around the table (Psalm 128:4).

I must clarify what this book does not attempt to do:

-It does not discuss state laws. An excellent resource to learn your state's laws is the Home School Legal Defense Association (www.hslda.org).

-It does not offer advice on how to inform your public school district about your intent to homeschool, if this is required by your state's laws.

-It is not a curriculum guide.

-It does not discuss, at length, why homeschooling is superior to mass schooling. Chances are, if you are reading this book, you have already researched the many benefits of homeschooling. If this book is the beginning of your research, then I recommend an excellent, concise book by David and Kim d'Escoto, *The Little Book of Big Reasons to Homeschool*.

-*School to Home* does not discuss, at length, educational or learning styles. Other excellent resources, some of which we list in the Additional Resources section, cover all of those subjects.

However, if you are a parent who feels that Christ is leading you to homeschool, *or*, if you have recently removed children from mass schooling and need encouragement, then *School to Home* is the book for you. You can and will succeed, by the grace of God!

The first chapter briefly covers the commencement of our own journey, and the following chapters provide practical recommendations to make your transition to homeschooling a smoother one.

Finally, Proverbs 17:22 says, "A merry heart does good, like medicine." Sprinkling your homeschooling journey with some laughter is critical. God later graciously showed us the humor in some struggles and situations that seemed bleak; those moments have inspired some of the cartoons in the book. We hope you enjoy them. Many thanks to my husband, Patrick, for his artistic work and for his general support.

May God bless you in your new endeavor!

Effie Damianidou Hill

(1)"The NAEP *Proficient* level represents solid academic performance for each grade assessed, with the ultimate achievement goal of all students performing at the *Proficient* level or higher. Students reaching this level have demonstrated

Introduction

competency over challenging subject matter. Thirty-four percent of fourth-graders, 30 percent of eighth-graders, and 21 percent of twelfth-graders performed at or above the *Proficient* level in science in 2009..."

http://nces.ed.gov/nationsreportcard/pubs/main2009/2011451.as

(2)http://nationsreportcard.gov/reading_2009/summary.asp

(3)http://nces.ed.gov/programs/crimeindicators/crimeindicators2010/ind_06.asp

(4)http://nces.ed.gov/programs/crimeindicators/crimeindicators2010/ind_09.asp

(5)http://nces.ed.gov/programs/crimeindicators/crimeindicators2010/ind_11.asp

(6)http://www.cbn.com/CBNnews/144135.aspx

(7)Wayne, Israel. *Homeschooling from a Biblical Worldview*. Covert, MI: 2000. Wisdom's Gate, page 10.

(8)http://nces.ed.gov/pubs2009/2009030.pdf

Chapter 1

"In their hearts humans plan their course, but the LORD establishes their steps." Proverbs 16:9

OUR JOURNEY BEGINS

I stood at the gas station in the frigid cold, waiting for the attendant to finish checking my tires. I had just dropped off our youngest child, of three, at preschool. "A flat tire...great!" I thought. I had the bottom-bulging tire filled with air and prayed that it would last until we made it to a repair shop. So off I drove, with a weighty heart and two teary-eyed children in tow. I tried to encourage my oldest son to crack open his books while we waited for my husband to pick us up from the tire repair shop and take us home. My son stared at me blankly, and refused. Thus began our first day of homeschooling. Not exactly the start I had envisioned!

The ensuing several weeks were full of tears and constant doubts whether we had made the right decision. During that initial period of transition, I often reflected, in disbelief, on the circumstances that had led us to keep our older two children at home.

We had, for years, toyed with the idea of homeschooling. We had even attended a relatively large homeschooling conference when our oldest child was just four years old. However, as life continued to throw one curve ball after another (the death of a parent, more babies, moving back and forth across the Atlantic to support my husband's career), we accepted sending them to private Christian school as a not-as-good, but acceptable, alternative.

That misconception was shattered halfway through our oldest son's fifth-grade year. Our daughter was attending the same school and was in second grade; our third child was in a nearby preschool. Since placing the oldest in private school, we experienced increasing reservations about institutionalized schooling for various reasons. The kids were encountering many of the problems we thought we would be avoiding by sending them to a private Christian school. Despite the financial investment, we found we were not getting a fair return. We still had to deal with negatives such as bullying, which the school often failed to address lest the offender's parents take offense, and they withdraw their child and funds; exposure to questionable games; non-Christian behavior, beliefs, and attitudes. Private Christian school was not the safe haven we had believed it to be.

We have heard many stories, too many to recount, of others who had come to the same conclusion. A close friend's first-grade daughter came home from her private Christian school, arguing vehemently that homosexuality was okay. Despite her mother's Biblical reasoning, the girl insisted it was true because she had heard so from other children on the playground. This example is just one of many that highlight the pre-eminence of what fellow students believe over what the parent says. My friend began homeschooling and, 15 years later, the girl is still wholeheartedly serving the Lord.

In addition, the generalization we had heard many times, that "problem" children were sent to private Christian schools to "sort them out," appeared to be true. Another downside to private schooling was our observation that the pace of the class did not always suit the pace at which a child learned, be it our child or a classmate.

The last straw, the one that finally broke our camel's back, occurred just before Christmas one year. A series of related events at the older two children's school, opened our eyes wider to the fact that only a parent genuinely has the best interest of their child at heart. Some staff members handled a building safety issue with such a lack of integrity and dishonesty that we simply felt that we could no longer entrust our children to their care. An even bigger surprise was the apathy of many of the parents! It was a particularly painful experience and decision, but after much prayer, we did not send our children back after the Christmas break.

There were many prayers and supplications on my part, asking God to guide us to another private school (we did have a couple of options). However, God in His ever-gentle but unrelenting way continued to speak to us to keep them home. With much trepidation I finally bowed my will ("for now," I thought), but with the understanding that I would homeschool until May, the end of the school year, and then "re-evaluate." This plan was easier than beginning at a different school halfway through a school year, I reasoned.

God had other plans. It only took a couple of weeks for us to realize that home education was not just a slightly better option, but a far superior one. We understood that it was the best lifestyle to live out Deuteronomy 6:6-7, by talking about, teaching, and esteeming the Lord's ways to our children. How does one teach God's ways to a student when school subjects are taught completely apart from God's truths? This occurs not only in the case of a public school setting, but

Chapter 1

Discipleship

in a Christian school environment, where "Christian education" often amounts to nothing more than opening prayer and sprinkling God here and there during the day. Such practices obviously do not guarantee that a school will impart a Christian worldview.

So, despite my double-mindedness during the initial weeks down the home educating path, I knew that God had indeed spoken to us to keep our children home long-term. Our third child joined us at the beginning of the next academic year. I often laugh that God "tricked" me into the decision to home educate, as it required some extreme circumstances for me to make that decision. I lacked the wisdom to take the jump myself. Our Father really does know best, as He uses everything to lead us down the path He wants us to take!

Many other issues with the private school surfaced once we kept our children home, and we started to sift through the effects. We had been paying a pretty penny for a "Christian" education only to discover that although Bible appeared as a subject, our daughter's teacher rarely taught it because she regularly ran out of time. The caliber of the other students' character was even worse than we suspected. Our children began to share with us stories of blatant, but concealed from authority, disobedience, blame-shifting, and deceit. Being young earth creationists, we were surprised to discover that one teacher taught, as an unquestionable fact, that God's creation was millions of years old. We were truly shocked to find that although our children's report cards reflected excellent grades, they did not have a grasp of the concepts corresponding to those grades.

What we learned from our painful private school experience was difficult, but invaluable in that it prepared our hearts to perceive the blessings of homeschooling. Nonetheless, the transition to home was not carefree or easy. Often, nothing worth doing is.

Your own reasons for deciding to remove your child from mass schooling might be similar or very different. Your initial hesitations, I'm sure, are the same! Some of these hesitations may be comparable to those that any parent considering homeschooling faces. However, when your child has been in an institutionalized school setting, there are some supplementary qualms: "Will my child adjust to this change? Will I adjust to it? Will we survive the transition?"

Chapter 1

I often wonder if it would have been easier to homeschool from the beginning of our children's academic careers, but I realize that God's grace is sufficient no matter where in our children's schooling journey we decide to begin to home educate them. My hope is that this quick guide will encourage others who are embarking on this fulfilling road less traveled. In the ensuing chapters, I lay out some simple principles that the Lord showed us, and I hope that they will be practical tools others can implement. You and your child can and will make the adjustment (and live to tell about it) with God's help, for "His divine power has given us everything we need for a godly life through our knowledge of him who called us by his own glory and goodness" (1 Peter 1:3)—even the divine power that will give us all that is needed for the godly lifestyle of homeschooling.

Chapter 2

"The righteous will flourish like a palm tree"

Psalm 92:12

TRANSPLANT SHOCK (Part 1)
EXPECT THE TRANSITION TO BE CHALLENGING

Some children ask to be homeschooled. The pressure of the academics in a rigid environment, the cliques, and bullying are just a few reasons I have heard. With the child that has an openness and willingness to be educated at home, the transition is greatly facilitated. In many cases, however, it is solely a parental decision.

For us as parents, and especially for me as the primary teacher, failing to be realistic about how challenging the transition to homeschooling would be was probably the one area in which we could have been more prepared. We had a fair amount of tears (theirs and mine), bad attitudes (theirs and mine), and questioning if this is what we were to keep doing (again, theirs and mine). God had told us clearly to keep the children at home, so, *"Why were the children not getting it? Why are they not embracing, with open arms, our new lifestyle?"* I would ask myself. Basically, they were suffering from "transplant shock".

Chapter 2

Transplant Shock

I have heard of home education referred to as the "greenhouse" effect. For a plant, the greenhouse provides additional warmth and protection, and ensures that the plants are strong enough and mature enough to handle the forces of nature, without being destroyed, when they are placed in outside ground. Similarly, children are like saplings that are to be raised in the controlled environment of a greenhouse (home) before being sent out into foreign soil (the world). They will have been raised under optimal conditions to strengthen them so that, when they are eventually faced with the challenges of a hostile environment, they will have the fortitude to not be destroyed by it. In other words, they will be properly equipped to be in the world, but not of it.

What if your sapling has already been planted elsewhere but, realizing that it is not the best soil, you have to dig it up to transplant it back to the greenhouse of the home? You must come to the conclusion that keeping your child in mass schooling will, in the end, prove to be more destructive than the temporary difficulties of making the move to home. However, transplanting a child from mass schooling requires some planning and care to minimize potential damage and to ease the transition.

"The righteous will flourish like a palm tree," (Psalm 92:12) was a scriptural promise that God gave us within the first week of our homeschooling journey. I knew that He was reassuring me that we would flourish in this new soil and lifestyle, to which He had led us. God often uses principles in nature to teach us spiritual concepts.

After all, God is the original "object lesson" teacher; just consider many of Jesus's parables.

I recently researched how to transplant a palm tree. (1) It is best to move the tree when the conditions are favorable, namely, in the spring or beginning of summer, when the soil temperature is getting warmer and the soil has been softened by rainfall. Discerning parents will look for the best time to move their child from school, and will take some time to adequately prepare the soil of their child's heart as well as that of their own hearts.

As parents, do your part by reading up as much as you can about homeschooling. Have the practical things sorted out—such as where, how, and when you will teach at home. Pray for peace and wisdom during your planning and commit it all to the Lord (Proverbs 16:3). If you can wait, plan to begin homeschooling at the beginning of a regular academic year. This will afford you the opportunity to have an entire summer to prepare yourself and your children.

Of course, there are extenuating circumstances, such as safety or bullying issues, where it is best to act quickly. In such cases, we recommend that you take some time off, at least a week or two, for a period of acclimation. Use this time to re-establish family connections by spending time together, by reading together, or by going on some fun field trips. This will yield good fruit in terms of children responding more agreeably when "formal" schooling begins.

Ecclesiastes 3:2 says that there is "a time to plant and a time to uproot." Ultimately, the Lord will point you to the right time to transplant your children to the home, be it mid-year, or the beginning of the following academic year.

Preparing Hearts for the New Soil

Despite any parent's best efforts, there will be a period of adjustment. I believe this to be the case because, first of all, children are just children. I remember distinctly, one day, the Lord prompting me to avoid the expectation that they will reason like grown-ups. Children will not grasp completely the long-term vision of homeschooling. My husband and I quickly realized the impact of multi-generational discipleship that homeschooling promotes. As adults, we saw the practical benefits it had in terms of academic achievement and the entire family's spiritual walk.

It can also be difficult for a child to accept that the same parents who enrolled them in a private or public school are now telling them that this is no longer the best method of educating them. After all, the same parents that have said they will always do what is best for their children, are now saying that they have a conviction that homeschooling is a superior choice.

We humbly explained to our children that we were, basically, not ready in our spiritual walk to do what we now believed to be more suitable, that is, keep them at home and educate them ourselves. Children tend to think in black and white terms. We explained that their years at school were not wasted and that there were some benefits, but that God had opened our eyes to a more beneficial way and we had to be obedient to Him. We also explained that home education afforded the best method to train them in God's ways. I'm certain that these thoughts gave them a lot of security. We were not merely following an arbitrary, spur-of-the-moment idea but we were executing a God-given conviction. It is important to let your children know that you, yourself, are under authority, and that your decision to home educate is God-led.

Children frequently live in the here and now. They care more about how something slightly negatively impacts them today, and less about how something will greatly bless them tomorrow. Children will benefit from parental wisdom and perceptions in this area. Share with them your thoughts on the benefits, as a tool to broaden their vision, and in a way that they will understand. For one of our children, an analytical thinker, we provided a brief history of public schooling. We also looked up great inventors and famous people who had been homeschooled.

For your own heart, if you cannot say that you have a God-given confidence to take the plunge, then don't give up yet! Even just thinking about homeschooling might be God's way of initially speaking to you. Educate yourself. Get books on the benefits of homeschooling. Speak to veteran homeschoolers. Examine the scriptures and, above all, pray! Ask the Holy Spirit to show you truth and to guide you, being willing to obey His leading even if it is not the answer you were looking for—as was the case with us, when we were initially so hesitant to homeschool. We soon discovered, however, that God had used the wisdom of homeschooling to answer our prayers to live a home life enriched with eternal treasures. "By wisdom a house is built, and through understanding it is established; through knowledge its rooms are filled with rare and beautiful treasures" (Proverbs 24:3-4).

Chapter 2

Severing Old Roots and Establishing New Ones

Children that have been removed from mass schooling to be home educated, will not usually embrace homeschooling immediately because they are emotionally invested in their former school and friends. They have had time to grow roots into their school environment—friends, teachers, schedules, the way the school does things. This was the case with our own children, to a greater degree than we had realized.

Accept the fact that you will spend your first year or two (and perhaps longer if the child has been in mass schooling for an extended time) adjusting and relearning relationally. This adjustment will be a bigger challenge than any academics.

In a plant, a gardener can minimize or even avoid transplant shock by disturbing the roots as little as possible, and by keeping them as moist as possible during the move. Experts caution gardeners to avoid bumping the root system or shaking the plant. How does this counsel apply to bringing children home? Discuss and explain your decision to them. Answer their questions. Be gentle and extend understanding, while remaining firm in your commitment to your new way of education.

Even though caution has to be exercised with the plant's roots, the gardener must sever the roots after a certain depth. Eventually, the roots to the old school system will need to be cut. Children will need guidance, time, and prayer to break the bonds they had before and to form new bonds. Old bonds to friends, teachers, and routines will eventually yield to new bonds to siblings, parents, and the new routine of home. We had our fair share of grief over the loss of their old way of life. This was the period during which it would have been easy to just throw in the towel. I was torn between feelings of irritation that things weren't going smoothly, and feeling sorry for our children's vexation.

Regarding friendship, children need to be encouraged to redefine it. We were open to maintaining some of their friendships from school, but it became a non-issue. In our particular case, few of those friends made an effort to keep in touch. As painful as this was, their silence spoke volumes to our children. We told them that we were now choosing to be more purposeful in relationships with others. We wanted to nurture high-quality friendships instead of ones of convenience, where children are friends merely because they attend the same school. In addition, the character of other homeschooled children spoke for itself and was a good "plumb line" for our children. They immediately noticed, and would remark on, the difference between interacting with previous classmates and these home educated children who were so nice, kind, honest, and accepting of others (no matter what the age gap).

Chapter 2

Furthermore, we saw the negative effect of school friendships on our oldest son's character. I originally thought that exposure to different standards would be a good learning opportunity; that is, it could open the door to discussions regarding Biblical standards for games, movies, other media, and personal behavior. We soon discovered that the school had not merely exposed our son to a counter-Christian viewpoint, but it had immersed him in it, and it was

Adaptation

starting to affect him. It took roughly two years of homeschooling before the light went on for him. One day, while he was doing school work, he commented that he had never realized how a previous classmate had been a compulsive liar and had gotten away with it. In reality, our son had nailed the problem with the latter part of his observation; sin (the lying) is no real surprise as foolishness is bound up in the heart of a child, but with no real accountability, it will remain there. Our son continued to share how his perceptions of his old classmates, and how they were disciplined (or not!), had now changed. Instead of pining for his "old school-going days" he had grown enough in godly wisdom to accurately discern, in a non-judgmental way, to what he had really been exposed at school.

Just as federal agents are trained to recognize counterfeit money by only viewing real bills, children who are immersed in godly living and Biblical training at home, will learn to discern counterfeit Christianity. In addition, Jesus admonishes us in Matthew 7:16-17 that we will recognize others' genuine faith, by the fruit they produce.

We assured our children that God would provide new friends, and in due time He did just that—another testimony to His faithfulness. The "socialization" they now had was not man-driven: a bunch of unwise, same-aged children being together all day. Instead, their socialization involved fellowship with other like-minded people interested in honoring the Lord in their lives.

Overall, these changes in perceptions made it much easier for our children to build right bonds with us as parents, and with one another as siblings.

Chapter 3

You transplanted a vine from Egypt;
you drove out the nations and planted it.
You cleared the ground for it,
and it took root and filled the land.

Psalm 80:8-9

TRANSPLANT SHOCK (PART 2)
CHALLENGES FROM WITHIN

Homeschooling is not for the faint of heart. At a recent convention I attended, one speaker noted that the number one reason for giving up on homeschooling is a lack of "follow through." Armed with some foreknowledge regarding what to expect, counting the cost, and preparing as best we can for any hurdles, we can certainly rise to the occasion instead of succumbing to defeat. Some of the challenges arise from within the home as new roles are embraced, or from within a parent or child as they adjust to the new aspect of the home functioning as both a discipleship and academic learning center.

Chapter 3

The "New" Parental Role of Teacher

Many parents are intimidated by the prospect of educating their own children, because they do not feel equipped to do so. Modern culture has separated our children from us via institutionalized schooling, and has led us all to believe that "experts" are more qualified to teach than we are. If your child has been in school, then those feared experts had names and faces! However, the most recent research conducted by Dr. Brian Ray of the *National Home Education Research Institute*, points to a different reality: homeschool students with college-educated parents score only about 8 percentage points higher than homeschooled students with parents who only had a high school education. This is not a significant difference considering that public school students with college educated parents score 27 (in writing) to 35 (in math) percentage points higher than those students whose parents only have a high school education!

This data does not surprise me, nor will it surprise you after you've spent some time home educating. The parent is an effective teacher because it is concern and love for the student, and motivation to see him or her succeed, that makes a teacher a *good* one—not academic training. Personally, I had people tell me that I enjoy homeschooling because I was previously a teacher. True, I taught college-level French as a foreign language for several years and I considered myself a good instructor. In fact, I always received good evaluations from my students. However, since I taught at the college level, teacher certification was not required. I had no formal training in how to teach French, but I discovered what many homeschooling parents learn—I learned how to teach as I taught.

My previous teaching experience also underscored another truth: neither a teacher nor a student can do his or her best when the class size is large. I learned quickly that if I had to cover a certain amount of material in a class period, I could not call on the student that was struggling the most. I simply did not have enough time to hold up the rest of the students.

I have another point of reference, and will share it because, almost 20 years later, I still remember this particular case. One semester, I had a class of only four students. One girl had already taken this course and had scored quite poorly. She needed to improve her GPA and reluctantly decided to repeat the class. Her previous professor warned me not to expect this student to perform much better as the girl, simply, "did not have an aptitude" for language. As it turned out, this class was one of my all-time favorites. We got to know one other, and I had sufficient time to get through the material and answer the students' questions. We could also take the time to practice what we had learned. The girl passed the class with flying colors! Interestingly, the previous professor had a higher level of education than me, and more experience teaching. I am certain that part of this professor's shortsightedness was due to conditioned thinking that class size is not a big issue; instead, the student, solely, was blamed for her poor performance.

Anyway, although I am a foreign language teacher, I am definitely not a math, history, geography, or any-other-subject teacher. There are many areas in which I was not comfortable instructing my children, academically speaking. My ability to teach is also hampered because English is not my native language and I was not educated in the United States, until college.

How do you teach a child to read English when it is not your mother language? I speak several languages and I have travelled the world, yet the thought of Kindergarten phonics caused me to break out in hives. I simply had not learned to read English with a phonics approach, and the concept seemed more than alien. My American history knowledge left much to be desired, and I honestly could not identify the presidents on paper bills or coins. Thank God for Kindergarten teacher manuals! Again, I soon discovered what many homeschooling parents realize: be willing to learn yourself, and you will learn along with your child.

There are many wonderful curricula out there, many with step-by-step instructions on how to instruct your child. If you really do struggle academically with certain subject areas, then soliciting limited outside help could be a solution. This discomfort can be especially true for certain high school subjects. A friend of ours briefly hired a former chemistry teacher to help her daughter through some difficult concepts. If finances are a concern, you can always barter with another person for services.

In addition, more and more curricula being offered are geared directly toward the homeschooled child. The suppliers know that there will not be an "expert" in a certain subject, in the traditional classroom sense. And many of these suppliers offer direct helplines. Many homeschooled parents have found that their children learn to find the answers for themselves, an invaluable life skill.

The Dual Role of Parent and Teacher

Even if the parent embraces their role as teacher, some still struggle with balancing their function as both instructor *and* disciplining, nurturing, etc. We tend to believe that these two roles are mutually exclusive. A parent or child might view this challenge as a hurdle to overcome whereas it really just requires a shift in perceptions. Let me elaborate.

I once had a friend ask if I would feel guilty giving my child a bad grade. First of all, grades in the home do not have the pre-eminence that grades have at school, particularly in the elementary grades. The parent can more than adequately assess what their child knows and does not know without grading, because the parent is not teaching a couple of dozen children all at once. Nonetheless, I personally found that grading was a good motivator, and we wanted our children to develop test-taking skills.

So, I mulled over this question of "bad grades." I had no qualms at all about giving one of my children a low grade if that is what he or she had earned. Why? The hard things in life are better learned in the loving and supportive environment of the home. An undesirable grade at school, where the teacher would probably not take the time to assess the source of the problem, is not a good alternative. A bad grade at home with a loving, "How can we improve this?" is, on the other hand, a good thing. When one of our children does more poorly on, say, a math test, I point out that mistakes are merely tools to improve our lack of knowledge. Errors are invaluable; without them, we cannot know what we do not yet know.

Educational Qualifications Solved

Correcting a child about a math error is no more painful or difficult than correcting a child about lying. But our culture has fragmented our lives. We are conditioned to consider one type of correction acceptable by the parent, but another type unacceptable. This is why I question the wisdom of parents who say they could never homeschool because they don't think they could fulfill the roles of both parent and teacher, or they express doubt that their child would accept being taught by them. I have heard these arguments more times than I can remember.

But what makes a mom think that if her child resists learning grammar from her, that same child will respect what she has to say about weightier matters—be they ethical, moral or spiritual!? The primary teacher in the home and the child must embrace this "new" Biblical model. Society has done families a disservice by having separated, and thus having dismantled, parental authority from academics. Homeschooling takes obedience to Colossians 3:20, "Children, obey your parents in everything, for this pleases the Lord," to a new level!

Again, I learned this truth first hand. I was relatively comfortable instructing, and our children accepted it. However, our oldest son would occasionally point out that his math schoolteacher had a master's degree in mathematics (read: "and you don't, Mom"). I soon discovered that although I was not a master mathematician, I was doing a better job. There were obvious gaps in his math comprehension as he had been taught to pass tests, not to grasp math concepts. So, we went back to the drawing board, going so far as to start his math book all over again, until he was not just jumping through the right hoops but really understanding the foundational ideas. This necessary redo did not make my son happy, especially since math was his least favorite subject.

There were several months where I felt that we were having a tug-of-war. I often felt that the battle was not so much for his math education but for his heart, and the real problem lay with a resistance to the authority that God had placed over him. It was a battle in his soul to implicitly trust God with his parents, and with the decisions that they were making for him. Finally, our son swallowed his pride and submitted to what I was trying to do. Did he suddenly love math? No, but his academic performance in this subject improved dramatically. So did his attitude. In the end, we both learned a deeper lesson than some math principle: no expert can replace parental care, and God blesses submission to God-given authority.

A mom I met recently had removed her three daughters from public school, and she identified that, initially, discipline and accepting instruction from her was a big challenge. She and her husband prayed and persevered, but eight months passed before their children became compliant. This mom wisely pointed out, "you do the hard work now, and things will get easier. But if you don't do the hard work now, things will just stay hard."

When looking at the New Testament, I was surprised to find how many times Jesus was referred to as "Teacher." There was an acknowledgement of Him being a teacher from the Pharisees, the people, Himself, and His disciples (for just a few examples, see Matthew 12:38; 19:16; 10:24; Mark 10:35 respectively). Granted, this refers to Him as a spiritual teacher; however, this same gifting to instruct that is in Him is, I believe, available to all of us through the Holy Spirit. The mandate in Matthew 28:20 to not only make disciples but to *teach* them to obey all that Jesus commanded applies to all of us. If Jesus entrusts us with this mandate, and of course we start in the home with our own children first and foremost, then He must assume we can instruct through the enabling of the Holy Spirit.

But, you might say, teaching our children about God is not the same as teaching algebra! Chances are, you have at least passed high school math and will be helping your child with concepts you have already studied. In any case, being good at algebra does not qualify you to teach it. My husband and I laugh sometimes when we recall some of our college professors. Patrick has an engineering degree and one of his professors was a genius in his field, but everyone knew that he could not teach. When children are on their own schedule, they learn to figure things out for themselves—self-directed instruction. Many times, one of our children has called me for help, but when I arrived (and they didn't wait too long), I found that they had processed the information and found the answer themselves.

If you are a parent, then you are also automatically a teacher. *What* you are instructing is really secondary. The same strategies can be applied to various subjects, and they usually begin with a proper assessment of the student. As a parent, you are the most qualified to assess what your child knows or doesn't know, as well as how they learn best.

From early on, you have taught your children to tie shoes, to ride a bike, to brush their teeth. You have a teaching gift. You received this gift the day you received that precious child. As any homeschooling parent realizes, the academics are not what is of the utmost importance. Bonding with your child so that he or she will be receptive to other instruction from you, is what is vital.

Perhaps when considering the parent as teacher, the real issue is not whether a parent will make a good teacher but whether he is a good learner. Many parents, products of the public school system themselves, have never developed a true love of learning. Any individual should consider education as an ongoing, lifelong process. There is always intellectual benefit to learning, but from a Christian viewpoint, we should always want to continually expand our understanding of God and His creation. After all, we are commanded to worship the Lord God with all our mind, as well as heart, soul, and strength (Mark 12:30).

If you can grasp this Biblical vision and goal, you will be willing to learn with your child. Your own love of learning will become contagious, and you will be "doomed" to succeed!

You may find that this transition from parent to teacher will not be as difficult as you think. Our eldest child told me something interesting about this subject, as I was his teacher briefly in a private school setting and he made no bones about disliking it. He pointed out that when education is in the home, a mother is doing the academic teaching but she is primarily still a mom—just a mom who happens to be teaching. In a school setting, the mother teaching her own child, appears to be a primarily a teacher and not a mom. This made him very uncomfortable. I think my son was trying to say that a mom who teaches in the home is natural, and teaching will appear to be a natural extension of what she does; after all, it's a God-ordained role for the mom, and now it is extending into the area of academics. In the end, therefore, the child will adapt to it.

Finally, many mothers themselves might struggle with this new role because they view it as a thankless job. They may grieve the loss of a sense of achievement if they were working outside the home. Reworking the finances can also be a burden, if the teacher gave up a paying job. The loss of free time is also difficult.

The antidote to these struggles is to focus on the eternal, rather than on the temporal. A friend forwarded me an anecdotal story about a woman who read a book on the great cathedrals of Europe and the lessons she learned from it. In this story the author writes,

"No one can say who built the great cathedrals—we have no record of their names. These builders gave their whole lives for a work they would never see finished. They made great sacrifices and expected no credit. The passion of their building was fueled by their faith that the eyes of God saw everything. A legendary story in the book told of a rich man who came to visit the cathedral while it was being built, and he saw a workman carving a tiny bird on the inside of a beam. He was puzzled and asked the man, 'Why are you spending so much time carving that bird into a beam that will be covered by the roof? No one will ever see it.' And the workman replied, 'Because God sees.'" The writer of the book on cathedrals went so far as to say that it is unlikely that anyone could build a cathedral in our lifetime, because so few people are willing to sacrifice to that degree.

We, as well as each of our children, are being built together by God into an abode that will bring glory to Him—"And in him you too are being built together to become a dwelling in which God lives by his Spirit" (Ephesians 2:22). As homeschooling parents, we must realize that we are being asked by God to be coworkers with Him. As we sacrifice the time and energy, and look to God for wisdom, we are doing the eternal work of carving, fashioning, and molding little souls for His eternal purposes.

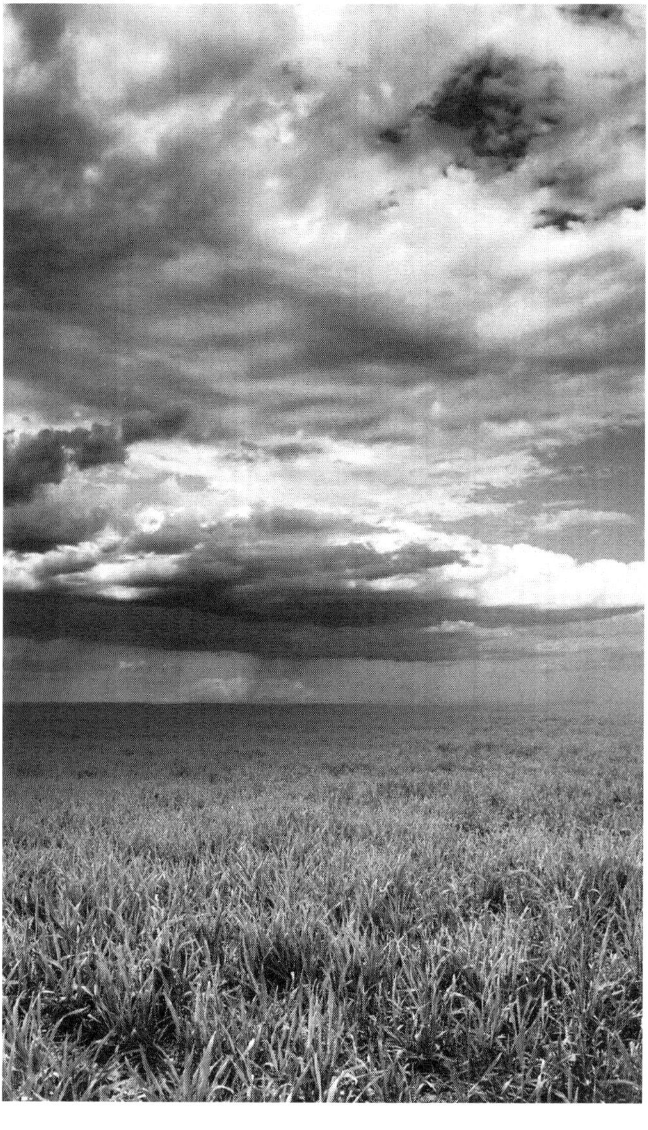

Chapter 4

By wisdom a house is built,
and through understanding it is established;
through knowledge its rooms are filled
with rare and beautiful treasures

Proverbs 24: 3-4

TRANSPLANT SHOCK (PART 3)

CHALLENGES FROM WITHOUT

As we reassess our perceptions of home discipleship and how it is linked to home education, we will prayerfully gain wisdom to fill our homes with God's eternal truths. Having our identity as teaching parents rooted in Christ, we become more secure in our calling to home educate. Still, there are some hurdles from without: others' opinions, our children now interacting with people of all ages, and the temptation to compare ourselves with those "other homeschooling families who are doing things so much better than we are!"

Chapter 4

Dealing with Friends and Relatives

Since we had considered, but opted out of, homeschooling when our first child was of school age, we had friends and relatives that felt at ease to tell us what they really thought of homeschooling. None of it was positive. Anecdotal horror stories of academic failure, social rejection, and social retardation abounded.

Perhaps your experience is different, and you have friends and relatives that are very pro-homeschooling. If so, praise the Lord! We, however, heard the full range of negatives. So, when we announced that we were actually pulling our children from institutionalized education to homeschool, we were generally met with a stunned, but polite, silence.

We knew what they were thinking about our new choice. They had felt the liberty beforehand, in the safety of the fact that our children were *not* being homeschooled, to give us their opinion of homeschooling. Such criticism can be intimidating for both parties. It is disquieting for others to see someone they thought held the same beliefs they did, do an about-turn and actually start homeschooling.

Do not feel like you are on a witness stand, and that you have to defend your decision. If there is a genuine interest from friends and family to understand your reasons, then there are many tremendous resources that adequately explain the benefits. You can either direct them to these, or arm yourself with some facts. Take it as an opportunity to educate the other party to the overwhelming Biblical basis of your choice. Have some statistics at your fingertips as well; it is difficult to argue with quantified facts gathered over several decades.

Unlearning the Pecking Order

For a previously mass-schooled child, another obstacle to overcome might be learning to interact with multiple age levels. Someone who is naturally gregarious, or who has not been in mass schooling for a long period, might not find this too challenging; but many children do. They have not had the opportunity to interact as often with adults, or with children who are younger or older. They've had more time, in mass education, to develop the stereotypical attitudes: disdain or superior feelings toward younger children, and fear or inferior feelings toward older children. Providing simple guidance for these social situations via an explanation that people are not segregated by age in the real world, may be all that is needed. It is also beneficial to admonish a child that he or she can be a good example to younger children, and does not have to cower before older ones.

I often reminded my oldest son, who had been in school the longest and who had some bad experiences with bullying from older children, that the Bible says: "Don't let anyone look down on you because you are young" (1 Timothy 4:12). This verse would include other children that are just a few years older! In the end, the best cure is continuous exposure. As a child has more opportunities to interact with other adults and youngsters, in varying age groups, which will come naturally while homeschooling, pecking-order thinking will become a thing of the past.

Have Realistic Expectations for Yourself and Your Children

Eventually, I gave up trying to compare myself with others who seemed to "have it more together." God has created each one of us with unique gifts, talents, and strengths. However, we also have unique weaknesses. I was more tired and stretched than I had been in a long time. The house actually looked lived-in now, and when it was cleaned up, it did not last for long. "Me" time was redefined, and relationships changed. I no longer had as much time for some of my hobbies and friendships. The time commitment to homeschooling seemed all-consuming.

Some of these changes are good and should be embraced. Pray for wisdom in areas where you feel "too" stretched. For example, I quickly realized that since we were all home now, the house would be messier, so more rigorous boundaries needed to be established. It was not okay to take something out and not return it (eventually) to its proper place. Although our children really embraced the extra time they had in the afternoons to just play, we quickly determined that additional daily chores, completed before that new extended free time, were essential. Chores offer a great opportunity to instill a good work ethic, and to teach children that as members of a family, they must contribute for the mutual benefit of all.

It was tempting, at times, to do a task myself rather than to teach my children how to do it, because it was often not done to my standards. So I lowered my standards of perfection and upped my level of commitment to instructing our children on how to complete a task—in a timely manner, not sloppily, and with the right attitude.

But the fact that I often had to address a child's bad attitude was also a deterrent for me to invest the time to show him or her how to do a chore. After all, rolling of the eyes when given an instruction does not constitute true obedience; authentic obedience is actually doing what is asked, doing it in the right time, and with the right attitude. All three components must be there.

Older women in the Lord, thankfully, encouraged me with the truth that the initial effort to teach a child how to clean a bathroom, for example, would eventually pay off. I once heard that, *"To be successful you have to suffer first, but you will suffer much more if you are not successful."* In other words, the initial investment requires more effort, but in the end, there will be an abundant reward.

We will reap the benefits of children who are quick to obey, who will do a job well, and who will do it with the correct attitude—not resentful, but being obedient from the heart. These are lessons that go far beyond just learning how to take out the garbage. These are didactic moments that prepare a child's heart to genuinely submit to, and ultimately follow, the Lord from the heart.

Chapter 4

A Word on Boundaries

Via homeschooling, I discovered a whole new world of resources, books, and websites that offered help for my home educating adventure. I soon discovered, however, that I had to set boundaries for myself, personally. When I continued researching information well into the night, to do a *slightly* better job in a certain area, I would soon burn out.

It's All Relative

Put a cap on how much or when you do things; for example, no more homeschooling preparation after 3 pm. Take time to rest before tackling laundry, dinner, and other obligations. It's okay to take that much-needed rest time. Not for selfish, "I need my time" reasons, but realizing that you will better minister to your family as a rested mother, teacher, and wife, rather than one who is on edge.

(1) ehow.com. "How to Transplant a Palm Tree."

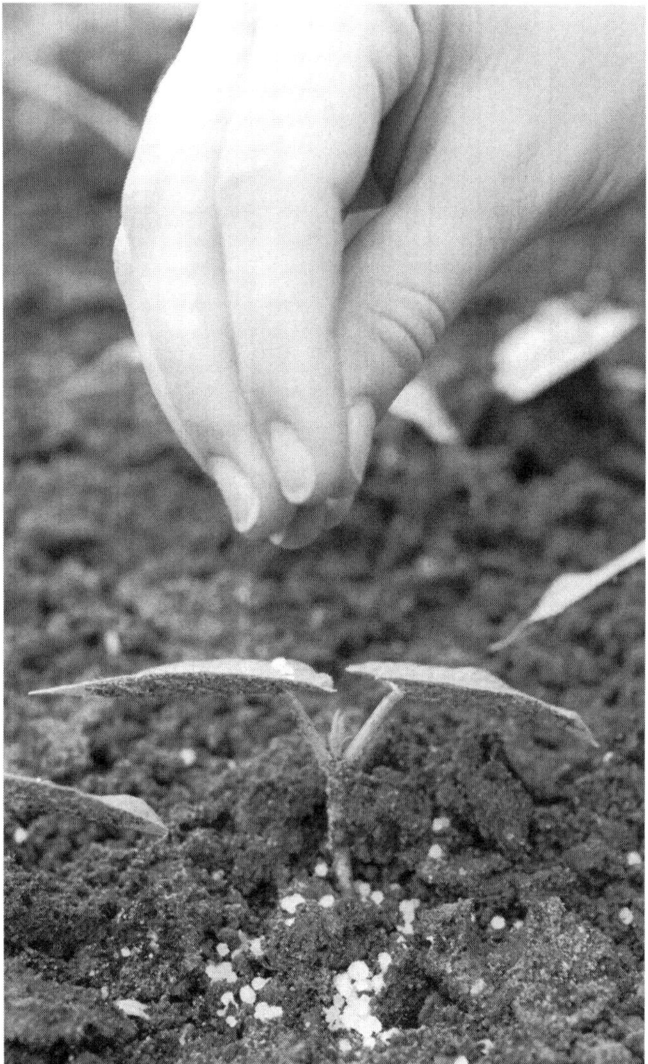

Chapter 5

Bless the LORD, O my soul, and forget not all His benefits

Psalm 103:2

Blessed be the Lord, who daily loads us with benefits, The God of our salvation. Selah.

Psalm 68:19 (NKJV)

ADD SOME SUGAR—HELP THE CHILDREN SEE THE BENEFITS

Another interesting gardening fact is that studies have shown the recovery time for transplant shock can be accelerated by giving a plant a simple sugar and water solution after transplanting. The solution may even prevent transplant shock if given at the time of transplanting. (1)

I distinctly remember the dazed look of our children during those first few days and weeks after we commenced our homeschool journey. How can we, as parents, help during this transition period? How can we add some sweetness to their souls to minimize the transplant shock of moving from mass schooling to homeschooling, and perhaps even avoid it altogether?

Proverbs 27:9 states, "Oil and perfume make the heart glad, so a man's counsel is sweet to his friend" (NASB). We are, of course, not primarily our children's friends; but this verse reminds us that good counsel is sweet to the soul. Our counsel in regard to pointing out the wisdom of homeschooling as an educational choice, and the counsel of prayerfully imparting Biblical truth to our children will go a long way toward nurturing them during this change.

Impart the Counsel of the Benefits

As mentioned in chapter two, children are still developing their spiritual perceptiveness. We cannot expect our children to reason the way we do. Perhaps obviously, they do not have the base of experience to think maturely in all areas, as they just haven't had the same opportunity to exercise discernment. Discernment comes with practice as we take events in our lives before God, choose to see things from His perspective, and modify the attitude of our hearts and our actions accordingly. "But solid food is for the mature, who by constant use have trained themselves to distinguish good from evil" (Hebrews 5:14).

Our wisdom can really help our children adjust. It's not a matter of adding an artificial ingredient, as with sugar water for plants; rather it is a matter of wisely pointing out the sweet benefits that the Lord has already put in our lives. If they're old enough, explain to your children your decision to keep them home. Help them see God's hand in it. Show them, from Scripture, the basis of your decision. Our children felt they had had positive experiences in their mass schooling, and it was sometimes confusing to poignantly point out all the faults of institutionalized education. We found it more constructive to highlight the benefits of a one-on-one education that was Holy Spirit-led.

We shared with them, in very simplified terms, the statistics of how home educated children outperform their public school counterparts in academics, social skills, and college performance. You can expand even further, of course, on the academic benefits of homeschooling, for example, tailored studies of their favorite topics. Whenever possible, let your children contribute to decisions regarding what they study and the family's curriculum choices. This involvement will lead them to sense automatically at least one benefit of homeschooling; unlike mass schooling, your family has the flexibility to choose what you study and how you study it.

I could expand on all the advantages to highlight, but it is best to pray that your children see for themselves the specific-to-them benefits of being at home. God will be faithful in this! The Word says that the Holy Spirit leads us into ALL truth (John 16:13), even the truth of home education and our belief that it is God's way for our family. His ways speak for themselves. After a couple of months, and of their own accord, our children made comments such as, "I had forgotten what it was like to play," "Wow, it's nice to not have to wait for everyone else to finish their work," "It's great to do some of our schoolwork outside in the backyard," "We're more of a family now," and "It seems like we're friends now." We took these positive comments as an opportunity to point our children to the Lord's faithfulness to them. We reminded them that even though we sometimes do not understand from the outset all the advantages of a path toward which He is directing us, we must still trust Him. What a faith-builder it was for our children to see the benefits of God's choice for them!

Impart the Counsel of God's Promises

Do you have any favorite Bible promises? They could be about God's guidance, how God sets the godly apart for Himself, or how He has called us to be a royal priesthood for Him. Prayerfully ask the Lord to show you how these beautiful promises can be better or further fulfilled by homeschooling. Then, share this wisdom with your children. It will be sweet to your children's souls.

Perhaps you have some scriptural promises that specifically pertain to homeschooling. We shared with them particular scriptures that the Lord had given us. We began the very first week of homeschooling by delving deeper into a specific promise the Lord had put in our hearts from His Word, regarding the children and homeschooling:

"The righteous shall flourish like a palm tree,
He shall grow like a cedar in Lebanon.
Those who are planted in the house of the LORD
Shall flourish in the courts of our God." (Psalm 92:11-13)

Instead of going straight to the textbooks and worksheets, we took time to read about palm trees, their uses, and what they represent biblically. Our children wrote a research paper and we made dioramas of an oasis with palm trees in the desert. We encouraged them with God's promise that as they grew in the soil of the home, where Jesus had planted them, they would flourish like palm trees. Palm trees are extraordinary in that every part of them is useful in some way. We encouraged our children that as they submitted to God's path for them in their education, God would make them useful in His kingdom.

Isaiah 54:13 says, "All your children will be taught by the LORD, and great will be their peace." Whenever possible, I pointed out when the Lord divinely orchestrated learning moments for them. For example, we had wanted to obtain eggs to incubate and hatch, but were unable to do so because of a local quota system. But within a few days of our initial disappointment, a robin made a nest and laid three beautiful eggs in a flowerpot right outside our kitchen door. We relished the opportunity as we would peer through the glass and announce, to whoever was not yet in the know, the fledglings' current stage of development. I have heard other homeschoolers testify to this sort of divine coordination of learning moments. Praise the Lord for them!

Keep a Record of the Benefits

How easily we, as humans, forget the Lord's blessings. Because we are forgetful, the psalmist encourages himself in Psalm 103:2, "Praise the LORD, my soul, and forget not all his benefits." In the Old Testament, God repeatedly admonished the Israelites to remember

Chapter 5

> Wow! At school, I never used to get a kiss when I finished an assignment!

Motivation

His deliverances and blessings. This can be done formally by record keeping, or informally by speaking of His blessings.

An avid scrapbooker, I made a "homeschooling" scrapbook. This was my personal way of remembering the Lord's blessings through home education. I begin each school year by taking pictures of our children on the first day and placing them in my scrapbook. I take pictures of interesting projects and field trips throughout the year, and also add them. I even recorded the robin's eggs in my scrapbook. It's a wonderful testimony and reminder to our children of the fun they've had while learning.

Your record keeping methods might be different. It could be as simple as mentioning the blessings when you or your children are having a hard day. Perhaps you can take pictures and simply slide them into a plastic photo album. Let your children pick and display their favorites, even cellphone pictures will do! You might keep and display crafts and projects they have made. Perhaps take pictures of these crafts and projects instead, and place them in your album.

A side note on the fun of learning: learning at home is very different from the regimented style of school. In a school, learning was either fun or serious. It was seldom both. Much of what you do at home will be fun and relaxed, but all of it is serious. There is more opportunity for hands-on learning. After all, people remember 20 percent of what they read but 80 percent of what they do. There is a naturally relaxed atmosphere that results from home education. After all, you can lie on the couch and do your math, or read a book in a tree house! A previously mass-schooled child might easily adapt, or he may have trouble with this concept. In any case, the natural atmosphere of home learning really is a benefit, and should be portrayed as such.

We have pointed out to our children some of the resistance and difficulties to homeschooling we encountered, but mainly as a learning tool. We have a real enemy of our souls who will do anything to oppose believers who are willing to sacrifice to draw closer to the Lord. However, the benefits are also real, and we would do well to remember them: the time to pursue real interests, more time to play, weekly lunches with dad, hot lunches at home, quality play dates, and so on. Previously, field trips were a rare privilege; now they are common, and we enjoy them just as much. And the icing on the cake in our household: for years the children begged us to get a dog, but we declined because they were in school, and I was afraid of being saddled with the primary care of the pet. But with the extra time garnered by home education, we finally consented to getting a dog. She is still a source of joy to our children, and they actually enjoy taking care of her.

Don't let me fool you into thinking homeschooling is a 24/7 rosy picture. We still have struggles and problems to work through; in fact, we have more than I would like. However, the benefits outweigh the effort by a large margin.

For many homeschoolers, their theme verse is Deuteronomy 6: 5-9. It encourages us to teach the Lord's ways as we sit at home or walk along the road, as we lie down and get up, as we enter or leave our homes. Have you noticed the blessing of that obedience in Deuteronomy 28:6? "You will be blessed when you come in and blessed when you go out." What a unique privilege we have as a homeschool family; we now have the opportunity to experience God's blessings together, as a family. At times, we just need a little reminder of this fact.

I sometimes overhear our children telling one another, "Hey, if we weren't homeschooling we wouldn't be able to do such and such." Eventually, the blessings become self-evident. In the beginning, just speak the truth and trust God to do the convincing. He will be faithful!

(1)http://www.gardeningknowhow.com/problems/learn-how-to-avoid-and-repair-transplant-shock-in-plants.htm

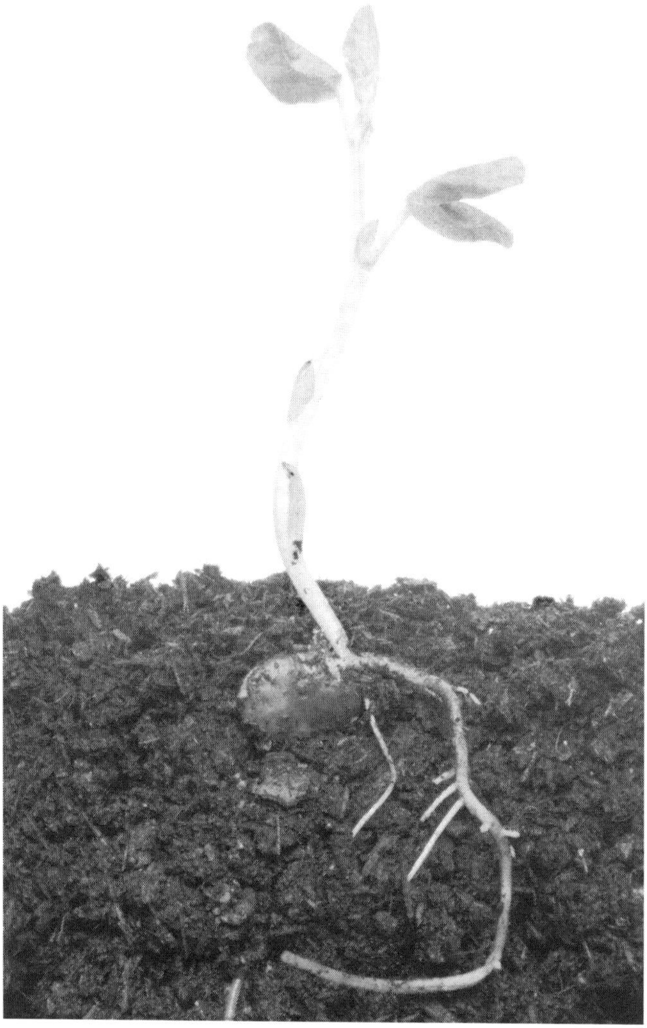

Chapter 6

Does a farmer always plow and never sow?
Is he forever cultivating the soil and never planting?
Does he not finally plant his seeds—
black cumin, cumin, wheat, barley, and emmer wheat,
each in its proper way, and each in its proper place?

Isaiah 28:24- 25

ACCLIMATION—ADJUSTING TO THE NEW SOIL

As a gardener diligently prepares his soil for planting, we too must prepare the soil of the heart and home for transplanting from mass schooling to the home. There will be weeding: Biblically addressing and removing bad attitudes, fears, and misconceptions. There will be spiritual plowing: preparing your heart and the children's hearts for the journey ahead. There will be practical plowing: where to school, how to do so and when, which curriculum to use.

Finally, the time arrives to place the plants in their proper place. The shift to homeschooling has been made. You are at ease, waiting to see the harvest of righteousness in character, academics, and family life to which other homeschoolers have attested. But wait! These plants are wriggling! They were familiar with the previous soil and preferred some of its aspects over those of the soil in which they now reside!

A period of acclimation is needed—the process by which a living thing adjusts gradually to changes in its environment. This process is generally not lengthy, but in the case of a child's acclimation to homeschooling, it can be trying for the parent.

Interestingly, I read that, "While the capacity to acclimate to novel environments has been well documented in thousands of species, researchers still know very little about how and why organisms acclimate the way that they do."(1) I really believe that God has placed this divine ability in all living things. In the case of homeschooling, the process will look different in your home than it did in our home, but following are some things we learned that will hopefully help you along in your journey! Ultimately, however, cling to the promise that God will show you the way that is best while adapting: "I am the LORD your God, Who teaches you to profit, Who leads you by the way you should go" (Isaiah 48:17).

Dealing with Comparisons

If your children adjust to and embrace their new lifestyle with ease, you are truly blessed. Our children were compliant, for the most part; but, like all children, they tended to gravitate to the familiar. It was natural that they compared what was being done in the home to what was done at school, for that is all they had known. These comparisons are part of the acclimation process. "We used to say The Pledge of Allegiance every morning," "I used to do math first," "My teacher told me to slant my B's this way." When hearing children's comparisons, the temptation to imitate their previous school format or environment increases even more. "Perhaps I should buy a little bell and ring it for recess," "Should I buy school desks?" "Should we wear uniforms?" These are all questions I have heard new homeschoolers ask. But beware of bringing children home only to replicate a school environment in the home.

In the beginning, these comparisons were very difficult for me. Our children frequently scrutinized our new methods. It was easy to take any comparison as a personal affront. But instead of getting irritated, or, worse, becoming insecure, it is best to listen to what your children want to say......*for a little while*. Gently remind them that this is how things will be done now, and that God will bless their endeavors at home.

With an attitude of grace and mercy on your part, *expect* obedience. First, expect obedience of yourself. God finally convicted me that hiding in the mudroom and telling my husband on the phone, through gritted teeth, that I could not/would not homeschool one more day was not exactly setting a good example of "Trust and obey, for there's no other way, to be happy in Jesus but to trust and obey." One day, God spoke to my heart that enough was enough. He was not talking about my children's whining; He was talking about mine. I humbly apologized to my children for my bad attitude.

Second, expect obedience of your children. Once my own heart was set on the right course, it was much easier to deal with the children's hearts. Once I embraced the fact that we were in this situation long-term and that complaints and negativity would only make it more difficult, homeschooling became easier. I specifically remember addressing one child's complaints with a simple, "God said this is what we are to do, and this is what we are doing until He speaks otherwise," instead of with appeasement and reassurance. That day was a watershed moment in our homeschooling journey. The whining, complaining, and pushing back disappeared almost overnight.

A Note on the Tongue

The area in which I fall short the most readily, is in the area of bridling my tongue. I am still a work in progress! However, it really is vital to order our speech aright during acclimation, as it will go a long way with helping the family adjust. Otherwise, an unbridled tongue can cause a lot of damage.

When I consider what the Lord has shown us regarding the negative effects of whining and complaining, from parent or child, I think of the Israelites of old. They did not enter the promised land because of their unbelief and their bellyaching. They grumbled about God's provision, His timing, and who would be leader. Homeschooling is not the promised land; however, it is a spiritual journey, and God uses it as a tool to fashion us and our children into the image of His Son. That is the promised land! At this place, we encounter the rest of abiding in God's blessing and provision for us. Like the Israelites, an unbridled tongue (which is, in reality, a reflection of what is in the heart) will keep us from reaping the benefits of the promised land in the area of home education: the strengthened family bonds, a sharpened awareness of the Lord and His leading in our schooling, His blessing upon our efforts, and success in discipleship.

I have been present when a child, resentful of having been kept home, has publicly humiliated his parents. The parents met cynical comments—about homeschooling and how their child longed to go back to "real school" —with discomfort and feeble attempts to reassure their child that this educational alternative was better. This scenario had little to do with homeschooling; rather, it reveals the rebellion in that child's heart that would have been expressed in many given situations. Homeschooling is merely another choice a parent has made for their child. Again, rebellion to that decision is just the tip of the iceberg. Would you let your children ridicule you about, say, the choice of profession that the spouse working outside the home practices (in other words, your choice of how you earn money to feed them)? Is it acceptable for your children to question your choice of where you reside (in other words, your choice of what puts a roof over their heads)? Will you let your children question you about the most important decision, homeschooling, which is actually a God-ordained method of education for Christian families?

The option to educate a child yourself is a big sacrifice, and this sacrifice can be pointed out to your child. The goal is not to lord it over him or her, but to demonstrate that he or she is so loved and cherished that you have sacrificed your time, resources, and finances (if income from working outside the home had to be given up). This should be reason for celebration and gratitude on a child's part, not a reason to begrudgingly accept it. Granted, having an attitude of gratitude does not come naturally to us humans; that is why the Bible exhorts us to give thanks sacrificially. "Therefore by Him let us continually offer the sacrifice of praise to God, that is, the fruit of our lips, giving thanks to His name" (Hebrews 13:15, NKJV).

Chapter 6

Homeschooling really is a gift and a wise gift-receiver does not look a gift horse in the mouth!

Creative Learning

Children will sometimes capitalize on a parent's insecurities. If you are not sure of your decision, or somehow feel guilty about it, your child will discern your indecisiveness. You need to resolve this issue in prayer and through God's Word before you enter this battle, or your home is liable to become a war zone.

Of course, it is completely acceptable for a child to voice reservations, fears, and concerns. There is also a godly way to appeal to authority in matters that are negotiable. There are decisions that are not black and white, such as which curriculum to use or in which extra-curricular activities to engage. However, in the end, expect compliance. There's a vast difference between a child asking questions, versus a child whining or complaining. The former can spring from childhood curiosity, a need to understand, or to be reassured. The latter behavior points to unbelief in God's provision, and thus to rebellion in the heart. Take this opportunity to address the real issues, and to learn to bridle the tongue.

A personal example of a godly appeal to authority was when one of our children initially insisted that he keep the exact same books he had used at school. We had hoped to make a break from strictly textbook learning, but decided that it would indeed be too much change all at once, and respected our child's wishes. The following year, we changed things a bit, and after two years, he was completely hands-off about curriculum decisions, since things had worked out well. Again, it was another occasion to point out to our child—not what super-parents we were—but God's faithfulness and goodness to him as we shared how we had prayed earnestly to choose what was best for him, in terms of curriculum.

At some point, we all have to learn to trust God through other people. Being homeschooled is a great avenue for a child to do so because, in the end, *they* will enjoy the fruit of *your* labor—a better education, more free time, and Christian discipleship.

Chapter 6

Facilitating Learning Styles in the New Soil

Children have different styles of learning, and there have been numerous books written about these. In the simplest sense, these styles can be loosely grouped into auditory, visual, and tactile. In addition, there are many different approaches to learning such as traditional, Charlotte Mason, Unit Study, Classical, and Eclectic. An excellent resource we originally used, that addresses both learning style and learning approach, is Cathy Duffy's *100 Top Picks for Homeschooling Curriculum.*

One benefit of homeschooling is the ability to tailor a child's education to his or her individual learning style. However, children who have been in mass schooling have not had this opportunity from the outset; no matter what their learning style, they have been forced to adapt to a traditional textbook-test approach to learning. They become used to the regimented approach needed when a teacher has 25 students in one classroom. A child removed from mass schooling may have a difficult time adjusting to a different learning approach, even if it is conducive to his or her true learning style. He or she may not immediately and easily adjust to, say, an exclusively Charlotte Mason approach, which advocates living books instead of textbooks as well as a large amount of outdoor learning.

The transition time will enable you and your child to identify his or her true learning style. Identifying your child's style doesn't have to be complicated. You will now have the opportunity to get to know your child in a different way—as a student—and it really is a blessing. I was surprised initially to discover many things about my own children that I had not known! I learned what interested them, what they thought, what they disliked. It was such a pleasure. Try different methods. Does your child enjoy worksheets, hands-on crafts, or lapbooks? Does he or she need to bounce on a ball while doing math drills? Discard what doesn't work. In the long run, it is not worth the wasted effort and extra stress of forcing your children to adapt to something that doesn't work, just to save some money spent on purchases!

Although you can now focus on your child's individual learning style, keep in mind that it is also not best to only teach to a child's strengths. Parents need to help their children to develop a bit in learning styles in which they are weak. This flexibility is a good skill to have when options are not so varied, as is sometimes the case in life.

Deschooling

In addition to handling comparisons, watching attitudes, and finding out how your child learns best, part of the acclimation process is adjusting to the home as the new learning milieu. This new environment will turn out to be an enormous blessing as it truly facilitates learning to a greater degree than a classroom. A child used to a classroom may need some time to "deschool." I am not referring to unschooling—an educational approach that emphasizes completely child-directed learning—rather, I am referring to a period of adjustment after removing a child from mass schooling, wherein their education was organized in pre-arranged time blocks, a rigid schedule, and regimented learning.

We found that some perks of homeschooling that others mentioned—such as sitting together on a couch and reading—were not always perks at the outset! One of our children was completely distracted when trying to do any schoolwork on a comfy couch ("I want to go to sleep"), or by windows with a nice view, and even by the bright colors in which our home is decorated. If this is the case in your home, train your child to shut out distractions: perhaps loosely time an assignment so that your child has a goal within which he or she must complete the work; change where he or she sits; turn off the ringer on the phone. Eventually, with your help, your child will adjust and these issues will no longer be as much of a concern.

We also discovered that in an institutional school, in general, children are taught to answer questions and not necessarily to think. I realized this challenge, more than ever, when I questioned my oldest son about some literature reading he had done. When he couldn't answer the questions, his response was, "Mom, I'm not really sure what you're asking me. At school, I would just figure out what it was they wanted to hear and then give it to them." Out of the mouths of babes! He had been taught to pass tests well, but not always to comprehend the information in depth. We have since had many meaningful conversations during which we rationally discussed why just passing tests cannot be the basis of a good education!

Another aspect of deschooling is breaking the spoon-fed habit. Many mass-schooled children tend to lack initiative, because they are given information, and generally do not have to work hard to obtain it. Put another way, children that have been removed from institutionalized schooling sometimes lack self-motivation in terms of taking ownership of their education. In many cases, they will not even know how to find topical, relevant information. They may not be able to, as is the case at home, let their curiosity lead them; home education affords the time and environment for children to naturally increase their knowledge by taking the initiative to look up something that interests them. Reading a fiction book set on a mountain might, for example, trigger inquisitiveness about mountains in general. A homeschooled child now has the time to look up facts on this subject: which is the highest mountain in the world, where is it located, what weather patterns take place on mountains? "Look it up!" has become an anthem in our home. A teacher with two dozen students simply doesn't have the time to let all of them independently look up information that interests them.

Take time to cultivate your children's initiative by giving them opportunities to look up required facts. For example, they can look up how to spell a word and what it means, instead of you quickly blurting out the answer. Make available a dictionary, a thesaurus, and other reference materials. Some of the best money we invested in homeschooling materials was spent on an electronic dictionary and thesaurus. I knew that our children knew how to flip through a book to find a word, but it really is faster for them to just type it in themselves. This efficiency spurred them to look up words they did not know. In addition, we bought a mini computer so that if information needed to be looked up, I could just point to the PC. Encourage learning in areas that interest them by keeping an interest inventory, and checking out related materials during your next trip to the library. I'm convinced that more real "education" has taken place via the questions that have sprung up during the day, than through the planned curriculum we are utilizing.

In addition to a general lack of initiative, children previously in mass schooling are used to most of their days being filled up with some sort of activity. A homeschooling friend told me that the hardest adjustment for her family, initially, was the lack of structure. At a public or private school, non-academic time is taken up herding children from one classroom to another, going to and from lunch, breaking for recess, and so on. Classroom time is not entirely productive either, as teachers answer the questions of only a few students that may not understand the material while the ones that do, wait. My eldest son's teacher would give him books to read since he was often the first to finish his work. She begrudgingly told me that she could not keep up with his consumption of books.

Others told me—and I experienced firsthand—that homeschooling did not fill an entire day because it is so efficient. Neither did I want it to. At the same time, I feared all the "spare" time we would have. What if our children fought a lot? What if there was a daily struggle for them to want to watch TV all day long? What if they grew bored, because not every minute of the day was accounted for?

Ironically, I found that our children fought a lot more when they were in school. I'm not sure why. I have heard other mothers echo this phenomenon. Perhaps they had previously bought into the pecking-order mentality. Perhaps they now had time to enjoy each other's company, or their primary interaction no longer occurred most often when they were tired and unwinding from school. Our children had now become each other's "classmates," and they embraced their learning time together. Anticipating the disputes I was convinced would occur, I actually bought a book on how to encourage siblings to get along. After several years of homeschooling, I have yet to open the book!

We removed the option of watching TV during our children's spare time, which eliminated that concern. We gave each child an allotted time for media, and that was that.

As for boredom? In her article, "The Benefits of Boredom," Wendy Priesnitz claims, "I propose that we reverse this fear of boredom because, in addition to negatively numbed minds, there are also constructively bored minds. If one is brave enough to hang out with boredom for a while (in oneself or one's children), they will find that boredom can be the great motivator and a push to develop one's inner self. Writer F. Scott Fitzgerald felt that boredom can be a tool for developing creativity. He wrote, "Boredom is not an end product; it is, comparatively, rather an early stage in life and art. You've got to go by or past or through boredom, as through a filter, before the clear product emerges.""(2)

The extra free time, initially, seemed strange to our children. At first they would mull around in the afternoons. Then our oldest son, with the most time in a traditional school setting, started to play with his toys. In his own words, he had forgotten what it was like to play! Interests, long tucked away under the stack of things that make a good little mass-schooled student, sprouted up again. He became engrossed in studying birds. We purchased a book on the birds in our state and a monocular. He took and printed pictures, and he started a folder of his findings. He also had time to play piano, one of his passions, at leisure.

No longer did our middle child fall apart in the afternoons, as she had when arriving home after mass schooling. She had needed time to "decompress" from the pressures of being in such a regimented environment surrounded by uncooperative children. The misbehavior of children at school had really frustrated her, and after keeping her home, I began to understand why. She was not judgmental or intolerant. I discovered she was extremely conscientious, to a fault at times, and she felt she could not do her best academically when the teacher spent so much time trying to keep the class under control. I also discovered that she was incredibly noise sensitive. At home, she became a voracious reader. It was a delight to see her face light up when she expressed an interest in something and had the chance to read about it, instead of hearing that we didn't have the time to do so. Trips to the local library became a much-anticipated weekly outing. The same child, very much a hands-on learner, blossomed under the freedom to do crafts and to be creative.

Make books and educational magazines available to your children, and watch how they gravitate to reading. Invest the time in some educational field trips and watch them begin to love learning. Take a trip to a local pond and put some of its water under a microscope. A whole new world will open up to them.

In summary, regarding the period of acclimation, be confident in what you know God has called you to do, especially when you don't measure up to their previous school in certain ways (and you won't). Realize that in no matter which way you fall short (and in some areas you will) when it comes to what is important, nothing in mass schooling compares to the well-rounded education you are giving your children at home.

(1)http://en.wikipedia.org/wiki/Acclimatization
(2)http://www.lifelearningmagazine.com/0408/benefits_of_boredom.htm

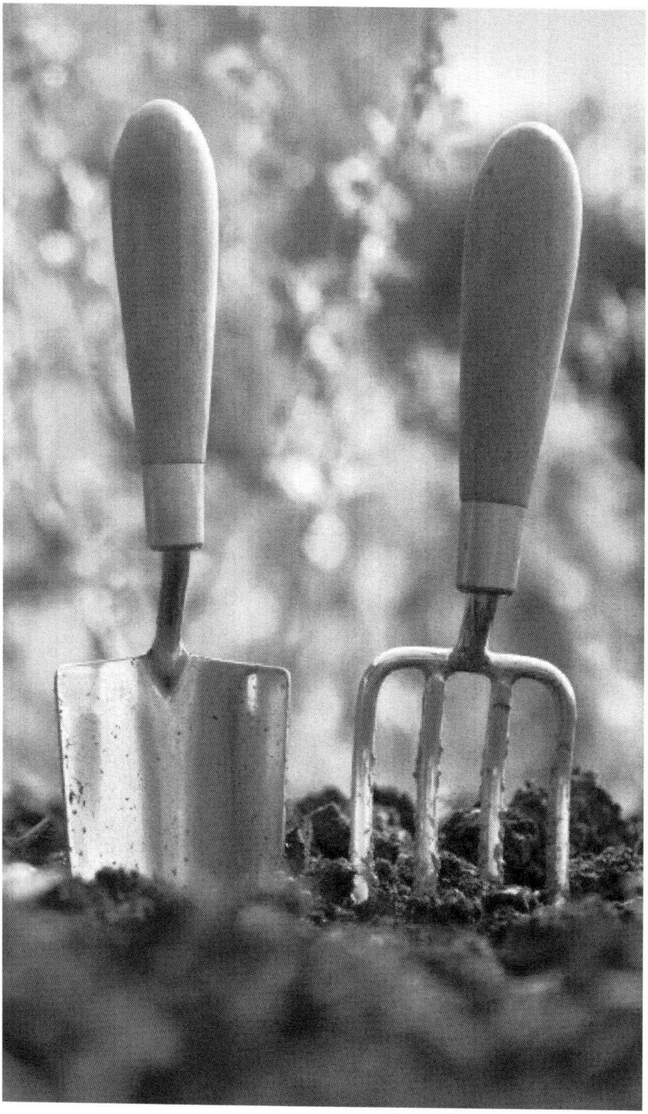

Chapter 7

Share each other's burdens

Galatians 6:2

ENLIST ASSISTANCE—GETTING SUPPORT

Instructions on how to transplant a palm tree, mentioned previously, also include enlisting the assistance of a few other people to help move the plant. For parents moving children from traditional schooling to homeschooling, outside support is essential. There are wonderful and insightful resources that will help impart a vision for your new journey, and that will strengthen you for the task ahead: books, magazines, state conventions, veteran homeschoolers, blogs, and support groups.

We joined a local support group, and it was a lifeline for us. It was so uplifting to discuss our struggles with others that had been on this path much longer than we had been, even when those people had homeschooled their children from the beginning. We discussed struggles with character training, choosing curricula, and schedules. The wisdom imparted to us was invaluable. I often felt that I was fumbling through it all; but those experienced homeschooling parents' insights, tips, and encouragement often shed light just where we needed it.

Initially, we naively believed joining the support group was mostly for our encouragement as parents. However, our children also benefitted tremendously in that they saw families on the same journey as themselves. At the same time, they realized that interaction with other children did not have to happen on a daily basis, as is the case in mass schooling. They embraced the truth that, generally, quality is better than quantity.

Going back to the palm tree analogy, the gardener must dig around the perimeter of the tree two and one-half feet down; any roots that have grown beyond that point must be severed with heavy-duty sheers. Ouch! Having to sever the root system children have developed into their previous school system can be painful, but it is necessary. Children that have been in a school setting are used to being around other children all day long. It can be a big adjustment for them to be at home all day with their siblings and with mom. The longer children have been in a school setting, the deeper they will feel this separation.

They will also be more mindful of "being different" now, since they are used to measuring themselves with other children who attend mass schooling. It is best to avoid the temptation to assure them that they are really not "different." Instead, affirm that yes, indeed, homeschooled children have been set apart—and that is a good thing, as the Bible instructs us to be in world, but not of it. Point out that, as Christians, we often face choices in life where we must go counter to culture. The sooner we develop the courage to do so, the better.

Many parents feel guilt for the anxiety that the change to homeschooling might cause, and for the loss of friends. Thus many mistakenly rush to compensate for these differences. What results is burnout, as they rush their children from one activity to the next. However, given adequate time and appropriate support, these challenges will represent a brief season in the transplant process.

Personally, we thought that getting outside help was essential, but that it should also be kept in balance. We resisted the urge to enroll our children in activities that would "fill the gap." In our hearts we sensed that, initially at least, it was important to somewhat limit outside interaction in an attempt to wean the kids from peer dependency. Old bonds had to be broken and new ones formed. There needed to be time for the roots to take hold in the new soil. That first year, we opted for no co-ops or supplementary classes. We all needed time to acclimate.

As time passed, and we became certain that we had planted the right seeds—ones of good bonds between them and us as parents, and among themselves as siblings—we did add some activities. Through our local homeschooling support group, we joined a parent-run co-op, participated in field trips, and attended park days. However, only after we were confident that we had laid a secure foundation in our children, did we think it prudent to start adding activities that we knew would enrich their home education experience and not compete with it. This period of "incubation" as I call it, did not last very long, but for us it was important to have.

Parents will have to exercise wisdom in this regard, because they alone know their children best. Some questions and honest evaluation would be constructive. How much support do I need? How much interaction outside of the home is advantageous and not detrimental to our homeschooling goals? Realistically, how much time spent outside the home is feasible or acceptable for our family?

Seeking Support

Whatever you decide to do—seeking lots of immediate outside support, or gradually adding support—make sure that a solid Biblical foundation is being laid in the home. Psalm 11:3 states, "The foundations of law and order have collapsed. What can the righteous do?" Many parents withdraw their children from institutionalized schooling and educate in the home because, in their hearts, they understand that a right and strong foundation must be laid in their children's hearts. Home education provides the best opportunity to lay that foundation for a life based on God's law and His order.

As 1 Corinthians 3:9-11 states, "For we are co-workers in God's service; you are God's field, God's building. By the grace God has given me, I laid a foundation as a wise builder, and someone else is building on it. But each one should build with care. For no one can lay any foundation other than the one already laid, which is Jesus Christ." We are to lay the proper underlying structure upon which our children are to build their lives—the completed work of Jesus Christ and living out the gospel, beginning in the home.

If you are unsure where to find support, begin by finding your state's homeschooling group. Its website or a quick phone call should point you to any support groups in your area. If there is a state convention, plan to attend. Visit your local library—most carry books and magazines on homeschooling. Finally, purchase books and subscribe to a magazine. Invest in yourself as the teacher! You are an important asset! Take full advantage of these helps as they will save you a lot of time, effort, and energy and will greatly aid you in making a smoother transition to homeschooling.

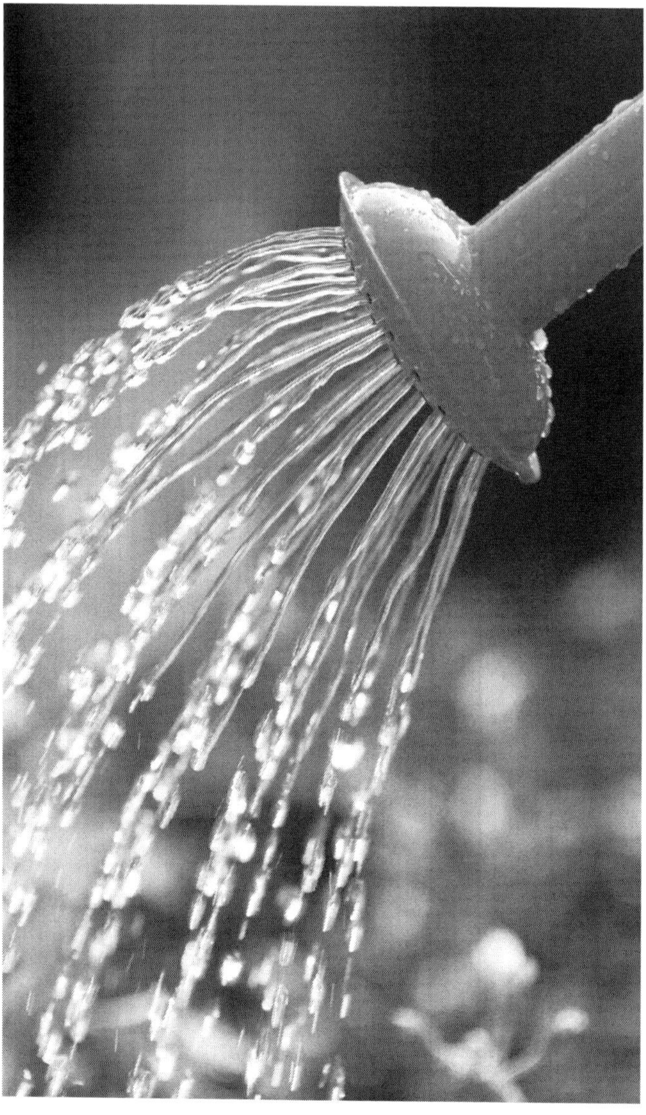

Chapter 8

But blessed is the one who trusts in the LORD,
whose confidence is in Him.
They will be like a tree planted by the water
that sends out its roots by the stream.
It does not fear when heat comes;
its leaves are always green.
It has no worries in a year of drought
and never fails to bear fruit.

Jeremiah 17:7-8

KEEP THE SOIL MOIST—NOURISHMENT IN THE HOME

When a gardener replants a plant in new soil, he or she must adequately water the roots to enable them to take hold. Sufficient drainage is vital, so that the plant does not sit in stagnant water. So too, we must continue to add fresh water, or life, to our homeschooling environment. In this way, we and our children will remain refreshed, and begin to grow and flourish in the home. Homeschooling is not primarily an educational pursuit, but one of faith. Faith, like a muscle, must be exercised to become strong. We, as parents, must put our faith to use in all areas of home education: how to discipline, which curriculum to use, how to overcome learning difficulties, how to keep the atmosphere of the home "moist" and rejuvenating. As we put our trust and confidence in the Lord, especially as we transition our children to home education, our efforts will be blessed and fruitful. He will show us how to keep those roots well-irrigated.

I think of grace as water, giving vitality where it's most needed. Initially, I had concerns about having the grace to deal with the rigors of home education. I was pleasantly surprised to discover that I had more grace to deal with my children when they were at home all the time. I usually have a "slump" mid-afternoon during which I feel depleted of energy, exactly when my children previously came home from school. At that time, they wanted snacks and needed to decompress from school, which often involved telling me about their day. Then there was all the homework. All I wanted to do was take a nap! I never felt that I was giving them my best.

With homeschooling, children no longer receive the leftovers of their parents' energy. There is a saying, "Where God guides, He provides," and it is true that He will provide the grace and wisdom needed on this new path. At times, when I've felt overwhelmed by the sacrifice that home educating requires, I reflect on the Israelite women in Exodus. Did God not understand that these women, who wandered through the desert, needed permanent homes? Did He not understand the frustration they must have felt as they finished hanging up the last wall picture, only to be told it's time to move again? Was He not mindful of the inconvenience caused by the continual uprooting? Well, I'm sure God did understand, but the higher purpose was more important—the purpose of taking them from Egypt's slavery to His promised land. Such is the call from the slavery of a humanistic agenda in public schools that will enslave our children, to the freedom of a Christ-centered home and future. God will not allow us to sacrifice our destinies on the altar of convenience. And as God miraculously provided water for the Israelites in the desert, He will refresh your soul as you pour yourself out to disciple your children. Furthermore, His Word promises, "He who waters will also be watered himself" (Proverbs 11:25, NKJV).

When educating at home, some watering is automatic. There is an atmosphere of richness as a family learns together. No longer fragmented, one family member's blessing will often spill over to the others. As one child grows spiritually and shares an insight, the others will benefit. As one child becomes passionate about a certain topic, his or her enthusiasm can be contagious. Even in practical academic learning, there is opportunity for mutual enrichment: if one child is doing an experiment or a project, another child will show interest and join in. This creates great bonding time between siblings. As we spend time together reading books aloud, or listening to a story on CD, our souls are somehow refreshed.

Following are some more practical points we discovered that helped us keep the home atmosphere a nourishing one. I pray that some of these will help you also!

Devotions

"The student is not above the teacher," Jesus stated in Luke 6:40. If we want to take our children's roots deeper, we will have to deepen our own. In homeschooling, there seems to be a natural process where this occurs, as the parent must dig to obtain answers for some of the pointed questions their children ask. Is the earth really millions of years old? Is evolution true? Is telling a half-truth ever okay? What makes a friend a good friend? The list is endless. I sometimes wonder what would have happened to those precious questions that arise so naturally during home education, had our children been amongst a group of twenty-some students.

Homeschooling transforms the parent. We have to live out our Christian walk in front of our children to a greater extent than if they were gone most of the day. Personal devotions become essential: how else do we tap into God's needed grace and strength? How else do we develop that essential sensitivity to God's Spirit?

During schoolwork one day I became angry with our middle child, and spoke very harshly to her. I then sent her to her room to think about what *she* had done. As I stood there, pondering what to say when she came back down, the ever-gentle voice of the Holy Spirit convicted me that I, myself, was behaving like a child. I called our daughter back down and apologized for my tone. Her face lit up. She had just been talking to the Lord, asking Him why parents don't have to apologize. Her heart softened and without prompting, she apologized for her part in the conflict. What a precious, Holy Spirit-rigged learning moment for both of us! This was great instruction in humility, forgiveness, and living out Christian fellowship in God's light; no Bible study could have driven these truths deeper. The Lord exposes sin in our own lives, and as we repent and embrace God's holiness, we hand the baton of eternal truths to our own children.

I soon realized that spending time alone in God's Word and in prayer sets a different tone for the day. This was also the case if I started school each day by first reading together from the Bible, and committing the day to the Lord. Sometimes we sing a praise song or two. A wise friend encouraged me to play worship music in the home. We will often play some in the background as we do schoolwork. Another benefit? I've discovered it's harder to yell at the kids when "Amazing grace, how sweet the sound, that saved a wretch like me," is playing in the background!

Before we began educating our children at home, we had devotions as a family, but not as often as we should have. At the outset of our homeschooling journey, my husband and I were strongly convicted to have regular family devotions. They had been at a Christian school before, but we could no longer say, "Not to worry, they are doing Bible in school." We could no longer say we didn't have the time. We are the ones primarily responsible for their spiritual welfare, and for some reason, deciding to home educate drove this point deeper.

Spending more time together as a homeschooling family does not mean that parents will automatically disciple their children. Discipleship has to be deliberate, but home education certainly affords more opportunities for discipleship, and for instilling a Christian worldview. I cannot count the times that God "turned on the light" for our family as we studied a subject.

One day, my oldest son voiced his opinion that having to study math was unfair—obviously not his favorite subject—and asked why he had to even do so. It occurred to me to point out that even if he

Establishing Traditions

does not eventually choose a career that requires much math, numbers point to a Biblical truth. Mathematical reasoning points to a God of absolute truth. Two plus two will always equal four. In this age of relativism, in which many hold that "if what you believe is true for you, then it's true," mathematics is a guiding light that exposes the fallacy of postmodern thinking. Absolute truth exists in many areas of life; we cannot say otherwise. Two plus two will never equal five no matter how sincerely I believe it.

Did my son suddenly love math? Hardly. However, I gave him some food for thought. I'm not opposed to studying Worldview separately as a subject; in fact, I believe just the opposite. But these types of naturally occurring moments, such as the one I just described, will fertilize the soil of our children's hearts in a much richer way.

Meaningful Traditions

Children that have attended institutional schools are used to some traditions at school. There are end-of-the-year field trips, Valentine's Day parties, St. Patrick's Day parties, and let's not forget pajama days. While I never wanted to compete with their previous school, lest I have the faulty motive of trying to imitate it, God put it on my heart to establish some Christ-centered traditions for our children. We need to celebrate for the right reasons, though. After all, we see in the Old Testament how God used feasts and celebrations to embed spiritual truths into the hearts of the Israelites.

We also read that Jesus was accused of being a glutton and a drunkard (Matthew 11:19). Clearly, this accusation was false; but Jesus certainly gave the impression of being someone that liked to socialize! In other words, we have a God that loves to celebrate. We have a God that is the Creator of the universe, and since we were made in His image, He imparts a measure of creativity to all of us. Pray for creative traditions to come to mind. Traditions don't have to be anything complicated; find things that will minister to the whole family in some small way.

In our family, we usually hold our "Beginning-of-the-School-Year Celebration" by going out for a special meal. Each child receives a small bag of new school supplies. We also usually hold an "End- of-the-Year Celebration." Throughout the year, as time allows, we will celebrate seasons, holidays, and birthdays with special field trips, crafts and other activities.

If you are not quite sure where to start, here are some very simple ideas to apply and prayerfully tweak to fit your family:

Beginning of the Year:

-The night before your first day of school, go out to a special restaurant.
-If finances are tight, choose a favorite meal to prepare at home, and to enjoy the evening before the first day.
-Purchase some fun, crafty supplies, and put them in bags for each child. Or, go out as a family to purchase school supplies, followed by a stop for ice-cream.

End of the Year:

-Enjoy a special meal or a dinner out at a special restaurant.
-Hand out gag awards:
  -Make simple certificates recognizing humorous achievements, such as "First Place for Wearing Pajamas the Longest Every Morning," "Loudest Pencil Sharpening Skill," and so on.
-Hand out real awards:

-Recognize greatest improvement in a subject, timely chores, excellence in pleasant speaking and tone, or exhibiting a certain fruit of the Spirit.

Valentine's Day:

-Make or purchase a simple foam mailbox. Display it in your homeschool area and write notes to each other during Valentine week.
-Decorate your school space with a red hearts garland.
-Make Valentine's Day cookies and cupcakes.

St. Patrick's Day:

-Cook corned beef and cabbage as a family. Make green hats to wear during the meal.
-Decorate your schooling space with a garland of green clovers.
-Check out and read a book about St. Patrick.

To Celebrate Servanthood:

-Make a "Helping Hands and Feet" tree:
On colored construction paper, trace and cut out templates of your children's feet and hands. Use a specific color for each child. Cut out a tree trunk from brown construction paper and a tree top from green construction paper. Attach the tree parts to white poster board. Whenever one of your children performs an act of service or kindness for someone else, write what that child did on a template of their hand or foot. Record events such as helping another child with a

subject, picking up after someone else, putting away dishes without being asked, and so on. Attach the template of the hand or foot to the green tree top. Display the tree with the various templates for all to see.

There are dozens of websites, magazines, and books that describe celebrations. One of my favorite books is called *Let's Make a Memory*, by Gloria Gaither and Shirley Dobson. The authors point out that special moments don't just happen; they must be planned. However, remember to avoid becoming so bogged down by the process of establishing these traditions, that you lose the joy they bring; keep it simple! A little will go a long way.

The most important thing to remember is that in Ecclesiastes 3:4, we are told "there is a time to weep and a time to laugh, a time to mourn and a time to dance and laugh." In verse 1, we read, "There is a time for everything." Well, there is a time to pick up the books and a time to put them down, and to make time to laugh and dance, and celebrate with your children! Between this truth and making time to pursue the Lord, you will have a steady flow in your home of nourishment for the soul and spirit.

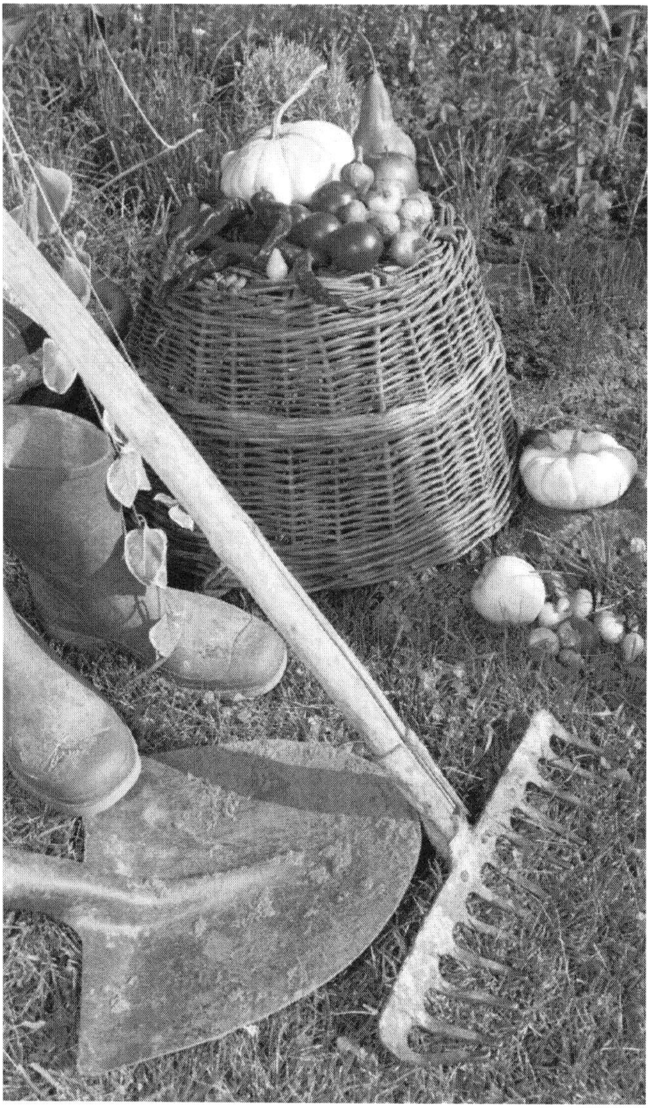

Chapter 9

I am the true vine, and my Father is the gardener

John 15:1

He who began a good work in you will carry it on to completion until the day of Christ Jesus

Philippians 1:6

See how the farmer waits for the land to yield its valuable crop, patiently waiting for the autumn and spring rains

James 5:7

CONSULT THE MASTER GARDENER AND WAIT PATIENTLY FOR THE HARVEST

No magic formula exists that will grant instant success in homeschooling. As with many things in God's kingdom, homeschooling is an investment in relationships. This is what God values most: our relationship with Him (vertical) and our relationship with each other (horizontal). Thus, our success hinges on a continued flexibility, sensitivity, and openness to the Holy Spirit to guide us in both of these domains.

In the context of educating and discipling our children, what works with one child, may not work with another. What works one year, may not work the next. We are forced to go before the Master Gardener, time after time, to ask Him in prayer what to do in any given predicament. Thus intimacy with Him is forged, as we go about His business of tending the garden of the home. What a wonderful privilege!

This principle of consulting the Master Gardener was saved for last so it won't be forgotten, since it is the most crucial element. After all, He knows the most about moving precious living things from one place to another. "You transplanted a vine from Egypt; you drove out the nations and planted it. You cleared the ground for it, and it took root and filled the land," we read in Psalm 80: 8-9. The Lord transplanted the entire nation of Israel, and He had to prepare the new soil.

God will give us guidance and wisdom through prayer, other people's counsel, resources, and His Word on how to remove weeds: bad attitudes, wrong thinking, incorrect judgments, or inaccurate perceptions. Similarly, He will teach us how to add nutrients that the family is to draw upon during homeschooling—how to choose the right curricula, iron out relationships, line up our perceptions in all areas (academic and relational) to His Word, have fun, tap into His grace.

Recording the Vision

Habakkuk 2:2 states, "Record the vision and inscribe it on tablets, that the one who reads it may run." As we prayerfully consider what the Lord wants us to accomplish in our homeschooling, it is very beneficial to write down your vision and goals. Many that have gone before suggest doing so, and they have proposed different ways to write down what you want to accomplish. Personally, I have found this goal setting helpful. It seems easier to become disoriented when children have been in a different "garden," or environment, as is the case when you are removing them from traditional schooling.

You have always been your children's teacher. However, the way you water, till, and fertilize this new ground is different. Basically, the way you interact with the children now is much more purposeful. Learning moments happen naturally. For example, questions on marriage, relationships, evolution, or life's meaning occur more frequently in the process of pursuing academics. It is helpful to have your vision embedded in your heart and mind to draw upon, when these opportunities arise. When they do so, although I often think to myself, "This is just not a good time to answer this question," I remember that we have certain goals in our vision statement, and this helps me. It spurs me on to take the time to answer the question and plant seeds of truth in my child's heart.

One of our children, for example, was reading through a creation magazine, and came across an article on the child sex trade. Our child had many questions, and although it was bedtime and we were all tired, I remembered that the Lord had given us certain goals for our children—to teach them compassion for others, and to pray for them to be an asset to the Kingdom of God. We took the time to answer the somewhat difficult questions and prayed about how to put God's love in action. We came up with the idea of making jewelry to sell, and a plan to donate all the proceeds to an organization that rescues children from the sex trade.

Your own vision statement can be whatever works best for you. If you are not sure where to start, you can prayerfully create goals in academic, physical, spiritual, and practical areas. Of course, there is overlap among these four, but this would be a good place to start. You should record some concrete ideas on how to best achieve those goals.

For example, under academic goals you might note that you want to develop a love of the classics and to understand artistic and literary expression that requires mature thinking and personal reflection. As to how to achieve this goal, you could note that you will choose curriculum that uses classical living books rather than "readers."

Under practical skills, you might note a goal of becoming self-sufficient in certain areas. Then, under how to achieve this goal, you could note that you will teach your children how to change a car tire, how to make jam, or how to grow vegetables.

These ideas are neither wrong nor right. It all depends on what the Lord puts on your heart, and what you as parents deem as important. It also depends on the interests of each child. Don't become overwhelmed with objectives; commit the goals you decide on to the Lord, and realize that it will take years to achieve them. Enjoy the process!

Stay Fluid

We tackled some issues with wisdom that God graciously provided. In the area of academics for example, our children no longer had other children to whom they could compare their grades and achievements—thankfully! However, those comparisons did motivate one of our children when previously attending a traditional school, so we prayerfully instilled a reward system: a little media time, staying up a bit past bedtime, and so on. However, we rewarded character, not scholastic achievement! Our children need to grasp this important distinction.

It was important for that same child to know that homeschooling was academically beneficial. I do not endorse standardized testing for all children, but we thought it wise to do SAT testing one year. Our child's superior results, which exceeded even his achievement at school, went a long way to alleviating any lingering doubts in his mind. For one child this sort of testing may be a motivator, for another child it may be something else. Again, the main thing to remember is that God will give us discernment as we ask for it, and He will guide us which path to take.

Since children that have been placed in a mass schooling environment have had plenty of opportunity and time to esteem teachers and peers above their parents, and since they have also had opportunities to pick up bad habits (read: sinful attitudes), it will certainly take time to adjust their thinking. Marilyn Boyer shared a principal that struck me and has changed my life: "If you have sown bad seed, God is just and you will reap consequences. But there is hope. In that same area, continue to sow good seed and in time, you will reap good consequences. "

Reaping the Rewards

As we continued to sow the good seed of godly authority, honoring God's Word as sovereign in all areas of life, and as we stayed consistent in child training and discipline, we began to see the fruits of our labor. Our children began to reason according to God's Word more often. They displayed godly character in new areas, and their hearts began to be knitted to ours. Just the other day, our oldest was reminiscing about some of his old traditional school days. Instead of speaking with longing for them, as often was the case previously, he marveled at how inaccurate his perceptions had been regarding certain issues. It is still an ongoing work, and many days discouragement crouches at the door. Still we know, "Let us not become weary in doing good, for at the proper time we will reap a harvest if we do not give up" (Galatians 6:9).

According to 2 Timothy 2:6, "The hardworking farmer should be the first to receive a share of the crops." This is what the Lord thinks of your hard work—in due time, you will reap the benefits of homegrown children. His Word promises it. If we do things His way, the benefits will be a natural outcome. We can either sow among thorns of a humanistic agenda at a public school, or the thorns of a religious but not necessarily Godly education at a private school, or we can sow among the carefully prepared soil of our home.

Children will draw upon the nutrients in their environment, just like plants will draw upon the nutrients in the soil in which they are planted. It can be soil with the theory of evolution, a Godless education, peer esteem, or the wholesome soil of God's truth and Word. In challenging times, I compare the sacrifice of home educating versus the alternative—the sacrifice of children that have been deprived of the best soil—and it puts things into perspective.

Homeschooling is a hidden treasure. However, until we roll up our shirt sleeves and dig for this treasure, it's difficult to comprehend and appreciate. Only after a bit of toiling do we experience for ourselves the hidden treasure of family bonding and discipleship, and the undercurrent of God being in control of our children's education.

The benefits then naturally manifest themselves, but initially it really is a leap of faith.

If, like me, you eventually discover the joys of homeschooling and regret having ever sent your children to school, be encouraged: God uses all things together for good. That sense of lost time can be a source of refocusing on the Lord, because He can redeem the time. Joel 2:25 assures us that He can redeem the years that the "locusts" have eaten. Now that we truly see the benefit of homeschooling, the past negative experiences are fuel for encouragement.

A final thought....

Deuteronomy 11:24 states, "Every place on which the sole of your foot treads shall be yours." What a wonderful promise! As we embark on the path of home educating our children, God promises to give us success. As we read in the Psalm below, He is ultimately the source of water, enrichment, the One that levels the rough spots, and Who provides the bounty in our homeschooling soil.

While it is true that transitioning from mass schooling to homeschooling poses many particular challenges, the end result, homegrown disciples of Jesus, is worth it. May God bless you richly in your new venture!

"You care for the land and water it;
you enrich it abundantly.
The streams of God are filled with water
to provide the people with grain,
for so you have ordained it.
You drench its furrows and level its ridges;
you soften it with showers and bless its crops.
You crown the year with your bounty,
and your carts overflow with abundance.
The grasslands of the wilderness overflow;
the hills are clothed with gladness.
The meadows are covered with flocks
and the valleys are mantled with grain;
they shout for joy and sing."

Psalm 65: 9-1

ADDITIONAL RESOURCES

D'Escoto, David and Kim. *The Little Book of Big Reasons to Homeschool*. Nashville, TN: 2007. B&H Publishing Group.

Duffy, Cathy. *100 Top Picks for Homeschooling Curriculum*. Nashville, TN: 2005. B&H Publishing Group.

Field, Christine. *A Field Guide to Home Schooling: A Practical Guide for Parents*. 1998. Revell Books.

Gaither, Gloria and Dobson, Shirley. *Let's Make a Memory*. 1983, 1994. Word Publishing.

www.hslda.org

www.nheri.org

Wayne, Israel. *Homeschooling from a Biblical Worldview*. Covert, MI: 2000. Wisdom's Gate.